POETRY

May 2018

D1365255

FOUNDED IN 1912 BY HARRIET MONROE

VOLUME CCXII · NUMBER 2

CONTENTS

May 2018

POEMS

VISUAL POEMS

FROM THE POETRY REVIEW

Editor	DON SHARE
Art Director	FRED SASAKI
Associate Editor	LINDSAY GARBUTT
Assistant Editor	HOLLY AMOS
Marketing & Production Assistant	HANNAH KUCHARZAK
Consulting Editor	CHRISTINA PUGH
Design	ALEXANDER KNOWLTON
Design Consultant	PENTAGRAM

POETRYMAGAZINE.ORG

A PUBLICATION OF THE
POETRY FOUNDATION
PRINTED BY CENVEO PUBLISHER SERVICES

Poetry · May 2018 · Volume 212 · Number 2

Poetry (ISSN: 0032-2032) is published monthly, except bimonthly July/August, by the Poetry Foundation. Address editorial correspondence to 61 W. Superior St., Chicago, IL 60654. Individual subscription rates: $35.00 per year domestic; $47.00 per year foreign. Library/institutional subscription rates: $38.00 per year domestic; $50.00 per year foreign. Single copies $3.75, plus $1.75 postage, for current issue; $4.25, plus $1.75 postage, for back issues. Address new subscriptions, renewals, and related correspondence to Poetry, PO Box 421141, Palm Coast, FL 32142-1141 or call 800-327-6976. Periodicals postage paid at Chicago, IL, and additional mailing offices. POSTMASTER: Send address changes to Poetry, PO Box 421141, Palm Coast, FL 32142-1141. All rights reserved. Copyright © 2018 by the Poetry Foundation. Double issues cover two months but bear only one number. Volumes that include double issues comprise numbers 1 through 5. Please visit poetryfoundation.org/poetrymagazine/submit for submission guidelines and to access the magazine's online submission system. Available in Braille from the National Library Service for the Blind and Physically Handicapped and from the Library of Congress. To request the Braille edition, call 800-424-8567. Available on microfilm and microfiche through National Archive Publishing Company, Ann Arbor, MI. Digital archive available at JSTOR.org. Distributed to bookstores by Ingram Periodicals, Media Solutions, Small Changes, and Central Books in the UK.

POEMS

For the Dogs Who Barked at Me on the Sidewalks in Connecticut

Darlings, if your owners say you are / *not usually like this* / then I must take them / at their word / I am like you / not crazy about that which towers before me / particularly the buildings here / and the people inside / who look at my name / and make noises / that seem like growling / my small and eager darlings / what it must be like / to have the sound for love / and the sound for fear / be a matter of pitch / I am afraid to touch / anyone who might stay / long enough to make leaving / an echo / there is a difference / between burying a thing you love / for the sake of returning / and leaving a fresh absence / in a city's dirt / looking for a mercy / left by someone / who came before you / I am saying that I / too / am at a loss for language / can't beg myself / a doorway / out of anyone / I am not usually like this either / I must apologize again for how adulthood has rendered me / us, really / I know you all forget the touch / of someone who loves you / in two minutes / and I arrive to you / a constellation of shadows / once hands / listen darlings / there is a sky / to be pulled down / into our bowls / there is a sweetness for us / to push our faces into / I promise / I will not beg for you to stay this time / I will leave you to your wild galloping / I am sorry / to hold you again / for so long / I am in the mood / to be forgotten.

CHASE BERGGRUN

From *"R E D"*

CHAPTER VIII

Tired   I walk toward everything except fear

over seaweed-covered rocks

I think that someday some new women

will be allowed to see each other happy

happy more than usual

I looked in all the other open rooms of my heart

A vague fear obscured the whole scene into a diorama of ruin

As sharp as a sword-cut   the light struck   a half-reclining cloud

Time and distance trembled in my body

•

To become in love with everything *apropos* of nothing

To see without seeming to stare

To change in the reflection

To appear peculiar

•

We never refer to sadness

as something that looks

like secrecy

but it does

•

I drifted on the fresh breeze

I did not like it

Joy   joy   joy   although not joy   a bad thing

I can feel it wet against my bosom

My journey is mapped and ready

I am only taking one dress

•

I don't want to talk   of infinitesimal distinctions

between man and man   see no difference   between men and maidens

I am the modern Morpheus
I made the minutes disappear
I am thin
an errant swarm of bees
a naked lunatic
faithful
selfish
old
a tiger
immensely strong
a wild beast

a paroxysm of rage
mercy
murder
coming
coming
coming

CHAPTER XIV

After a bad night I lock myself in my room and read

I had only imagination

I remember how on our wedding day   he said

I shall never let trouble or nervousness concern you   you can trust me

I must not forgive   I cannot

I know the real truth now

My imagination tinges everything with ill adventure

I suppose a cry clears the air   as other rain does

·

I have a good memory for details

it is not always so with young ladies   or so it had been said to me

I cannot comprehend this husband

Women all their lives are interrupted   considered hysterical

summoned to make children for the strong and manly

and for his sake must smile and not speak

Now this man I began to think a weak fool

I had trusted him   my husband

even half believed his words when he said

I would have an ordinary life   without dread

•

Let me tell you from experience of men

his brain and heart are terrible things

This man   impotent in the dark

He succeeded in getting me to doubt

everything took a hue of unreality

I did not trust even my own senses

You don't know what it is to doubt everything   even yourself

I am a wife he fashioned by his own hand

to be sweet and earnest and so kind

•

An idea struck me

Following great loss   people see things that others cannot

Men want to explain explain explain

see themselves new   pretend to be young

Ladies' bodies are deemed unholy

by the very men who burn them

Generations of men believe that women

walk amongst them without knowledge

My thesis is this

I want to believe   to believe

to believe in

a universe   willing

to understand

CHAPTER XXI

A detail in a pool of blood

the body gathered in an awkward kink

I dress myself in easy anything

●

I softened into a swollen confusion

only slightly solid   I was shining

He beckoned

His hands   a dark mass like a thousand rats

A cloud closed over my eyes

I moistened myself with brandy

I held tight to life

I became like water

●

Kneeling on the edge of the bed   his face was turned

his left hand   held both arms   his right gripped

my neck   blood   a thin stream of it   his nostrils quivered

●

I lay in disarray

my eyes   and from them came   an endless moment

Cold moonshine dazed me   I began to pull on clothes

I drew back   unclean

Shame folded me like steel   tried to twist me in obedience

I could not feel the rise of reddening dawn

Silence   the sound of what happened

·

I want you to know all this

understand   how much I need to show you

It was he who caused me to disappear

My husband   my husband and other men

hunt me and command   my flesh my blood my brain

This is my pollution story

·

The eastern sky became clear
        as the awful narrative deepened
            in the morning light
                    when the first red streak shot up my flesh

EDUARDO C. CORRAL

Testament Scratched into a Water Station Barrel
(Partial Translation)

After Rita Dove

Apá, dying is boring. To pass las horas,
                          I carve
              our last name
                  all over my body.
I try to recall the taste of Pablo's sweat.
                          Whiskey, no.
              Wet dirt, sí.
                  I stuff English
into my mouth, spit out chingaderas.
                          Have it your way.
              Home of the Whopper.
                  Run
for the border. ¡Aguas! The mirror
                          betrayed us.
              It erased your face
                  from my face.
Gave me mother's smile, narrow nariz.
                          Once, I wore
              her necklace.
                  The gold slick,
obscene. God, I was beautiful.
                          Cada noche,
              I sleep
                  with dead men.
The coyote was the third to die.
                          Your money
              is still in his wallet.
                  Quien engaña
no gana. Apá, there's a foto, in my bolsillo,
                          of a skeleton
              shrouded
                  in black flames:

Nuestra Señora de la Santa Muerte.

Patron saint
of smugglers, pick-
pockets, & jotos.
La Flaca. Señora Negra. La Huesuda.

¡Aguas!
An animal
is prowling
this station. It shimmies with hunger.
It shimmers
with thirst.
To keep it away,
I hurl my memories at it. Your laughter is now
snagged
on its fangs.
Your pain
now breathes inside its lungs. Taste
the feeling.
Siempre Coca-Cola.
America's
real choice — I gathered & smashed bottles.
Apá, follow
the glass
snaking from
the barrel to a mesquite to find my body.
Lips blue,
skin thick
with scabs.
Apá, kneel in the shade, peel

the scabs. Touch
our last name.
Solís.

Testament Scratched into a Water Station Barrel

                              In the desert, the moon
               shivers. Tonight, to stay awake, I'll cut my feet
with glass.
                         Outside Oaxaca, in a clinic, my mother said,
          "I hate your Indian face."
               In the dream I'm running. My limbs skeletal
and scabbed.
                         After my mother's death, I found, in a box,
          her wedding dress.
               As I lifted the lid, a stench corkscrewed
into my nostrils:
                         the dress had curdled like milk. During the day
          I gather tinder.
               Paper. Shed snakeskin. When the last light
above the mountains
                         knots into stars, I crouch under mesquite,
                                                  make a fire.
               Sometimes the moon stops shivering. Sometimes
          I tally what I owe.
                         In the dream I'm running through a hallway.
          The floor uneven.
               The walls green. Last month, as my son blew out
          the candles
                         on his cake, I noticed, for the first time,
          the hideous shape
                    of his nose. Tonight I'll pinch my thighs to stay
          awake. My mother,
                         in the clinic, said, "The rain has a fever, it
          needs plenty
                    of rest, it needs to drink plenty of water." The doctor
          scribbled in a file
                         then asked for more money. If my mother
          could see me now!
               My feet bloody. My face darker than ever.
          Tonight, to stay awake,

I'll sit close to the fire. In the dream I stumble,
but I never let go
of my right breast: an urn heavy with my own
ashes, an urn
I'm lugging God-knows-where.

RAYMOND ANTROBUS

I Move through London Like a Hotep

What you need will come to you at the right time says the tarot card I
overturned at my friend Nathalie's house one evening. I was wondering if she said something worth hearing, *What?* I'm looking at her
face, trying to read it, not a clue what she said but I'll just say *yeah*
and hope. Me, Tabitha, and her aunt are waffling in Waffle House by
the Mississippi River. Tabitha's aunt is all mumble. She either said
Do you want a pancake? or *You look melancholic.* The less I hear the
bigger the swamp, so I smile and nod while my head becomes a faint
foghorn, a lost river. Why wasn't I asking her to microphone? When
you tell someone you read lips you become a mysterious captain. You
watch their brains navigate channels with BSL interpreters in the
corner of night TV. Sometimes it's hard to get back the smooth sailing
and you go down with the whole conversation. I'm a haze of broken
jars, a purple bucket and only I know there's a hole in it. On Twitter
@justnoxy tweets *I can't watch TV / movies / without subtitles. It's just
too hard to follow. I'm just sitting there pretending and it's just not worth
it.* I tweet back *you not being able to follow is not your failure.* It's weird,
giving the advice you need to someone else, weird as thinking my
American friend said *I move through London like a Hotep* when she ac-
tually said *I'm used to London life with no sales tax.* Deanna (my friend
who owns crystals and mentions the existence of multiple moons)
says I should write about my mishearings, she thinks it'll make a good
book for her bathroom. I am still afraid I have grown up missing too
much information. I think about that episode of *The Twilight Zone*
where an old man walks around the city bar selling bric-a-brac from
his suitcase, knowing what people need — scissors, a leaky pen, a bus
ticket, combs. In the scene, music is playing loud, meaning if I were
in that bar I would miss the mysticism while the old man's miracles
make the barman say *WOAH, this guy is from another planet!*

Fish & Chips

I saw another ladybug
Chicago could win
if I eat the leftover fish & chips
in every line so I don't forget
We went to the river called fish & chips
We stayed at the fish & chips tower
They donated a million dollars to the fish & chips foundation
so we could go to school for free
It's called fish & chips college for women

PHILIP GOOD AND BERNADETTE MAYER

Alternating lunes

amaryllis comes in many flavors
snow sometimes slants
when will politics make improvements?

strawberry amaryllis walks right in
snarling at snowfall
saying flowers don't abuse women

female rabbi demands ancient answers
untranslatable tablets found
there's more knowledge in flowers

aren't all rabbis ancient females
snow's setting in
untranslatable strawberry soufflés, first course

ancient untranslatable second course arrives
edible flowers abound
distant whale sounds sing loudly

singing memories of the future
they thought so
singing, singing, never stopping singing

echo above sea level roads
people ponder protest
extreme weather patterns manifest warnings

swim swam have swum under
and in soufflés
until willows swill scotch seltzers

no tree left behind pleas
a branch fell
right into the money jar

no money have I none
neither do you
so together we'll be bereft

piles of words mound high
counting moon phases
feathers flew across our minds

consult the feather field guide
mostly about toucans
and birthdays and cookie monsters

we live in the country
they wonder why
the thin place is nearby

it's a wordy country here
full of vegetables
each word is a pea

lots of potatoes with eyes
carrots without tops
one frozen leek left behind

carrots have eyes too, y'know
you can sit
on a mushroom, never ginger

some folks sit on rocks
large, smooth, flat
and shakers made fine furniture

some rocks start to shake
like a quaker
I've never dated a dentist

dating a dentist really bites
tooth-growing oysters
what a very weird universe

s is a yellow letter
in my synesthesia
I mean my synesthesia scheme

can you hear sunrays?
see trumpet calls?
taste the shape of words?

if you spell synesthesia with
an *a* (synaesthesia) everything
changes because *a* is red

synesthetes come in many colors
snow sometimes slants
when will untranslatable make improvements?

if you stick with me
what everything does
will be the backwards opposite

improvements make untranslatable demand flowers
hear, see, taste
everything will make sense again

you've got another thing coming
I see people
nothing will ever make sense

nonsense to making sense again
the mysterious mind
memories within time plus space

do you know the future
will be there?
time might go backwards, sir

if only pleasure were limitless
beyond the mind
a tiny speck of sand

if only you knew how
limitless pleasures can
be like little engine dresses

yes the small pleasures roar
like mighty engines
here sometimes they are jets

you mean nuclear jet engines
like the speedway's
oh save us and the trees

more trees will save us
air moves through
we hear maple sap drop

trees taught us to breathe
sap rises up
we see windy voices say

nothing is really real tonight
the wind laughs
oysters jump on our plates

JENNY XIE

Ledger

The Sangre de Cristo Mountains mottled as if with oil stains. Configurations of cloud-shadows.

Easy gait of hours: a way through — or into — the dry winds.

Our church is the mountains, says the guide to the tour group, all of whom have been instructed to keep their cameras inside their bags. A group crowding the aisles of San Geronimo Chapel.

On the dirt path between adobe structures, bareheaded. Stretching, palms out, as steam from the boiling pot does.

To move along the earth without keeping a ledger.

The horsefly not so incongruous with the sagebrush. Still, reflexive swatting.

We're good citizens, we serve in the Army, though we're regarded as second class by the US government.

Framed badges and news stories in the house of the retired sheriff. Men in his family who have been policemen, firemen, soldiers. His wife pinching the ears of bear sculptures formed from mica clay.

Thick paste of red soil and the piñon that pierces through it.

To carry on from day to day without exercising the sloppy hand of manipulation.

Four dollars for a plate of fry bread in cinnamon butter. The boy at the counter restless, wanting to get back to the electronic dance music on pause on his iPhone.

Reading a history backward, the deep strata.

Settling on this life as a parasite on its host.

That man next door who you bought from? He sells jewelry made by an Anglo woman. His wife.

The stray dog asleep on her side, dreams ripped from her open jaw.

Money touched from hand to hand.

Whole lifetimes spent trying to make sense of an appetite.

A town called Tres Orejas. *Three ears*. Plenty.

D.A. POWELL

You Didn't Hear It From Me

the bare-backed barback
in the bear bar's back bar
barebacked with a bare bear
who was also a barback back there

Talk to Strangers

don't talk to stranglers
when yr wasted do
talk to swingers don't
talk to swindlers if
you can tell them apart
from the strangers who
are just strangers no
stranger than you alone
and afraid to be alone
cuz they might want
to touch your throat

Slut

spread millet in this neighborhood
all you get is bluejays

bluejay may be cooked three
ways

Orchestral Maneuvers in the Dark

I play the egg
and I play the triangle
I play the reed
and I play each angle
I play the lyre
and I play the lute
I play the snare
and I play the flute
I play the licorice stick
and I play the juke
I play the kettle
and I play the uke
who ever thought of the triangle
who ever thought of the clarinet
the castanets the cornet the
discotheque the harmonium
the euphonium marimbas and
maracas harmonicas
tom-toms and tatas
I play the fiddle
and I play the jug
I play the washboard
and the washtub
I play kalimba
and I play the koto
I play the organ
and I play the banjo
I play the fool I play it cool
I play hot and I play pranks
I played your mixtape
forgot to say thanks

Fledge

the pope has his cardinals
batman has his robins
shakespeare has a lark
in just one of his sonnets

Bible Belt

if you didn't mind the bible
you'd surely mind the belt

Tatt That

kiss
upon

kiss
they

grow
into

this
they

wish
your

shad
roes

hand
sock

hard
rock

cold
toes

will
blow

warm
will

blow
cold

they
just

raid
your

hash
then

like
meat

bees
with

your
cash

they
give

they
take

form
like

your
fist

over
love

Talk to the Undertaker

let's say you want flowers
you should have flowers

let's say you want forever
you should have flowers

let's say he should have
you in and out by tuesday

and if you want flowers
you should have flowers

and the flowers will stay
fresh until tuesday you say

yes that's the way it's done
should you want flowers

A Night at the Opera

turns out
there are no
dead bodies
after all
unless you
put them there

MATTHEW DICKMAN

Bluebells

Blue light ringing through
the green grass.

The bent heads of petals

are not praying
to anything or to anyone.

Only we are
standing in a field of them,

my son and me and me
holding him.

In my arms he stretches
out to the very far ends of the earth

like a radio signal

made of skin and organs,
of everything.

I was singing a song to him
I made up

about me dying.
Since yesterday he has not been

crying as much as screaming
like it is terrifying

to wake up.

It is terrifying to wake up
and terrifying to sleep

and his feet going blue in the cold
spring air

in which he is growing.
His mother is growing him

with the milk she makes all day,
spilling out in blue.

The song I am singing to him
puts him to sleep,

will put me to sleep.

Will one day burst the drum
in my ear

like a bell, very much like a voice
screaming from far off,

though you don't know
if it's hurting or hungry or nothing at all.

Fiddlehead Ferns

Olive seashells
in the air

you can eat.
The very inner of the inner ear

in the breeze.
Last night my son dreamt

about falling
out of trees.

I had almost forgotten
that we were

simians.

The fiddlehead turns
on itself but only ever in love.

Green cinnamon roll,
a snake too small to hunt

anyone.
Curled in like my son's
fingers, his fists.

More beautiful than
a spider fern,

spun-in island,
moldy tongue of a hippopotamus,

the eye of the forest.

When my son wakes up
screaming

I don't pick him up
right away.

I tell him where he is and who
I am.

At night all the fiddlehead
wants to do is sleep.

When I sleep
I dream about death adders curling

around his soft
body,

all of us making the same kinds of sounds.

Lilac

One look at the lilac, one smell
and my childhood is —

dogs scratching at the sliding
glass door, bits

of bottles coming up

like grass in the grass, a dirty towel
down by the feet

of the tree, Lysol cans, small
packets of Land O'Frost

turkey meat —
there in front of me in spring,

in the wonderfully fat rain,

flowering purple and whatever
the pinkish purple is called

and the white

ones too. They smell like
my siblings, like the backs of my infant

son's ears, like my son
whom I would kill someone for.

Before he was born I wouldn't kill
anyone. But now I would.

And after I'd get a coffee
from Starbucks, a coffee and a piece

of that amazing lemon-frosted
lemon cake

and think nothing of it,

and read the paper and hold him
against my chest

and listen to his body living,
alive outside

his mother's body, and the lilac
outside on the street, outside

everyone, and heavy in the rain.

NOAH BALDINO

Passing

The Ware Collection of Blaschka Glass Models of Plants,
Harvard Museum of Natural History

The ovaries, when splayed, resemble
        sliced tomatoes. Or rose windows,

each geometry precise enough
        to praise. I want to press my tongue

against the bloodroot petal, to run
        its stamen along my slick shelf of

teeth like a man might with a wheat stalk.
        Four times so far other tourists

have taken me for a gallery
        attendant. In the glass, a slow-

sidling crimson spreads over my own
        skewed reflection: a hesitant

teen in a Harvard hoodie, the fifth,
        leans in to ask, *Excuse me, sir?*

Are they really glass? — a testament
        to how my binder encases

my breasts, my faith in the plum yew's fruit-
        shorn frenzy. Dense clusters teeming

with their separate blossoms, any
        unknowing eye might think they were

living. But I know the lilac's tell:
        two blemishes, bulbous where some

hot glass mis-dripped, then caught forever
in the filament. Sometimes, I think

I'll wake to find they've finally
trickled off me in the night, pooled

molten down the bed and gathered
back again. I might thrash off both breasts

in a sleepless fit, or could unfurl
my clit like a pollen basket passed

from a honeybee's hind legs
to the hive. It makes its secret

seen. I can only answer yes. Yes,
They're real. I mean, they're *really glass.*

You could snap a stem between fingers
with such a slight force, one stark blink —

the flies flitting the gallery would fear
the weight of their own landing,

thick wings rapt still. When the public,
in their distressed astonishment,

demanded to know how the Blaschkas
transported the models without

a fracture in even one pistil,
Leopold Blaschka revealed his own

elaborate process: pack each
flower tightly in its cardboard

cradle, then strap them down with strong wire
                    to restrict movement, and set each, at last,

in a wooden box wrapped with burlap.
                    They drove them straight from Manhattan

in two hearses. The drivers, of course,
                    wore black suits. Onlookers parted

to allow their small procession past.
                    I like it here, with everyone

focused on the flowers. Hunched, kneeling,
                    as if suspicious, still doubting,

the teen eyes two tiny zinnias,
                    then moves on to another case.

I've seen many leave unsatisfied.
                    They can't bear to be partitioned —

how can I blame them? Someone made these
                    with their body. They let their breath

unspool to form each impossible
                    bud, crafted every flower's fold,

then waited on the heat to break to
                    hold just one, wearing special gloves.

Wouldn't anyone wish for just one lie
                    among a garden this precise?

One daisy swapped out in secret, switched
                    with a common courtyard flower,

now waiting for someone to notice
               its wilt while its counterparts keep

all their glisten. It does seem to me
               true punishment: never to change.

Unflinching forever. Sometimes, near
               closing, when the hall becomes quiet,

I really do believe they're real.

HENRI MICHAUX

Postface

"Plume," 1938

I have, more than once, felt my father "pass" through me. Which immediately raised my hackles. I have lived against my father (and against my mother and against my grandfather, grandmother, and great-grandparents); having never made their acquaintance, I have not been able to fight against my more distant forebears.

In so doing, what unknown ancestor have I allowed to go on living within me?

For the most part, I did not follow the beaten path. In so doing, what unknown ancestor's path might I have followed? What group, what ancestral average might I have followed? I was constantly changing directions, sometimes it was I who gave them the runaround, sometimes vice versa. A number of them barely had the time to appear in a flash, then to vanish. Some would only appear in a given climate, in a given place, in a given position, never elsewhere. So numerous, so rapid, so conflicted was their appearance — another major problem — that I never knew exactly whom to lean on.

One is born of too many Mothers. — (Ancestors: simple chromosomes, bearers of moral tendencies, what does it matter?) And then the ideas of others, of my contemporaries, everywhere telephoned through space, and my friends, my attempts to imitate or "to go up against."

I would have nonetheless wanted to be the respected head of a laboratory, to be someone considered as having successfully overseen the operations of my "self."

Dispersed, in tatters, I held my own, and there was never anybody in charge, or if there was, I immediately dismissed him. He irritated me right off the bat. Was it he who let me drop? Was it me who told him to get lost? Was it me who held myself back?

The young puma is born with spots. After which, he moves beyond his markings. This is the force the puma exercises against his ancestors, but he never moves beyond his hunger for meat, his playfulness, his cruelty.

For too many thousands of years, he has been dealing with his conquerors.

SELF makes itself up out of everything. A shift of inflection within a phrase, is this another self attempting to make its appearance? If the YES is mine, is NO a second me?

Self is never more than provisional (changing as it does when faced with somebody else, an ad hominem self changing when set in another language, another art), always bearing within it a new persona, a new character which the slightest accident, the slightest emotion, the slightest blow to the head will liberate to the exclusion of the previous self and which, to general astonishment, often emerges, formed instantaneously — therefore already having taken complete shape beforehand.

One is perhaps not made for a single self. One is perhaps wrong to cling to this. One takes unity for granted. (Here, as elsewhere, it is our will that impoverishes us, sacrifices us.)

In a doubled, tripled, quintupled life, one would be more at ease, less corroded, less paralyzed by the hostility of the subconscious toward the conscious (the hostility of all those other "selves" that have been dispossessed).

What wears one down the most over the course of a day or a lifetime is the effort and the tension necessary to maintain an identical self faced with the continuous temptations to alter it.

One wants too much to be someone.

There is no single self. There are not ten selves. *There is no self. SELF is but a point of equilibrium.* (One among a thousand others, always possible, always at the ready.) An averaged "self," a crowd movement. In the name of the many, I sign this book.

But was this something I wanted? That we wanted?

There was pressure (vis a tergo). A force from the rear.

And then? I threw it out there. I was somewhat disconcerted.

Every one of the tendencies within me had its own will, just as every thought that presents and organizes itself has its own will. Was this will mine? Many wills inhabit me, this person, that person, a friend, a great man out of the past, Gautama Buddha, many other figures, many lesser figures, Pascal, Ernest Hello? Who knows?

The will of the majority? The will of the most cohesive group?

I did not wish to be devoid of will. What I willed, it seems to me, went against myself, given that I didn't wish to will and that nonetheless I did will.

... Crowd, I managed as best I could amid the movements of my crowd. Given that everything is a crowd, every thought, every instant. Everything past, everything interrupted, everything transformed, everything is something else. Nothing ever definitively circumscribed, nor susceptible to being so. Everything: a relation. Mathematics, symbols, music. Nothing fixed. Nothing on the order of property.

My images? Relations.

My thoughts? But thoughts are perhaps precisely that which runs counter to the "self" — losses of equilibrium (phase 2), or recoveries of equilibrium (phase 3) within the movement of "thinking." But phase 1 (equilibrium) remains unknown, unconscious.

The true, deep flow of thinking no doubt takes place *without conscious thought*, and without image. The perceived equilibrium (phase 3) is the worst, the one which after a while strikes everybody as loathsome. The history of Philosophy is the history of the false points of conscious equilibrium that have been adopted in succession. And then: *is it by the tip of "flames" that fire is to be understood?*

Let's be wary of following an author's thought (even though this author be of the stripe of Aristotle),* let's rather attend to what he has in mind, what he is getting at, the mark that his desire to dominate and influence, however well hidden, attempts to impress upon us.

Besides, WHAT DOES HE KNOW ABOUT HIS THOUGHT? *He is quite ill-informed about it.* (Just as the eye knows not what composes the greenness of the leaf which it nonetheless sees with such clarity.)

He does not know the components of his thought; he might sometimes be aware of the initial ones; but the second ones? the third ones? the tenth ones? No, nor the distant ones, nor the surrounding ones, nor the determining ones, nor the "AHAs!" of his era (which the lowliest high school teacher three hundred years down the line will recognize as obvious).

---

*Thought is less crucial than the perspective from which it arises.

His intentions, his passions, his libido dominandi, his mythomania, his irritability, his need to be right, to triumph, to seduce, to astonish, to believe and make others believe in whatever he so pleases, to cheat, to deceive himself as to his appetites and his disgusts, his complexes and his entire life tuned, without his even knowing it, to his organs, to his glands, to the hidden life of his body, to his physical deficiencies, everything remains unknown to him.

His "logical" thought? Well, it circulates within a casing of paralogical and analogical ideas, a path striking out directly by cutting though circular routes, seizing (one only seizes by cutting) the bloody stumps of this so richly vascularized world. (Every garden is rough on trees.) The false simplicity of primary truths (in metaphysics), followed by an extreme multiplicity, which remain to be conveyed.

At a single point, willpower and thought flow together, inseparable, and falsify each other. Thought-willpower.

At a single point as well, the examination of thought falsifies thought, just as in microphysics the observation of light (the trajectory of the photon) falsifies it.

All progress, each new observation, each thought, each creation seems to create (along with light) a zone of darkness.

All knowledge creates fresh ignorance.

All consciousness, a new unconsciousness.

Every new contribution creates a new nothingness.

Reader, what you hold here, as is often the case, is a book not made by its author, even though an entire world went into it. And so what?

Signs, symbols, élans, pratfalls, departures, relations, discordances, everything figures within it — to pick oneself back up from the ground, to go on looking, to seek further, elsewhere.

Amid these things, refusing to settle down, the author grew a life.

Couldn't you also perhaps try to do likewise?

Translated from the French by Richard Sieburth

VISUAL POEMS

A Billion Things in One

God went
crowd-surfing at Kinfolk 94

clad in
Yeezy Boosts
God floated
overhead.

This is for all my ladies

she said

While few
may know   God
          her   followers
are

                                         often
                              celebrities

She   gets name-checked
in rap songs

          Which is fine.

This is what you see if you

follow

God

         God

     the always-on

the   #NeverNotWorking

            lit from below

          with

         an external

battery pack

called   Queen of

                Highsnobiety

voice of Generation Y
                'It' girl
the Millennial dream

Instagram

　　selfie　　God

　　　　　　　　　　　　never-

ending party

　　God

　　　　　　　God

　　　　　　with Disney

princess eyes

'What am I?   God

said

in

    h   e   r

turtle

                        down   coat

        I'm a

billion things in one

We are literally

you r

curren   c

y

sa

ng

a couple hundred

thousand people

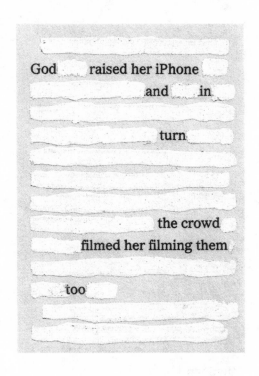

God raised her iPhone
and in

turn

the crowd
filmed her filming them

too

"A Billion Things in One" is an erasure of the article "YesJulz, Snapchat Royalty" by Max Berlinger, which appeared in the *New York Times* on June 30, 2016.

KINGA TÓTH

From "We Build a City"

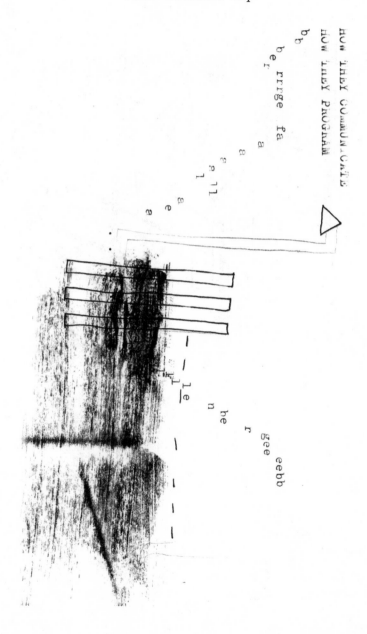

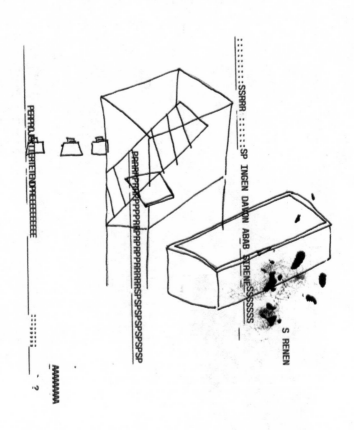

JOEL LIPMAN

Series of Pictures

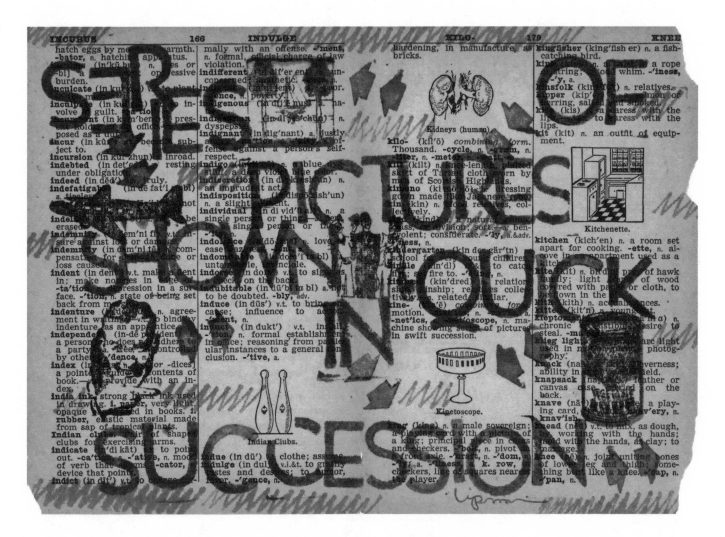

From "TEST"

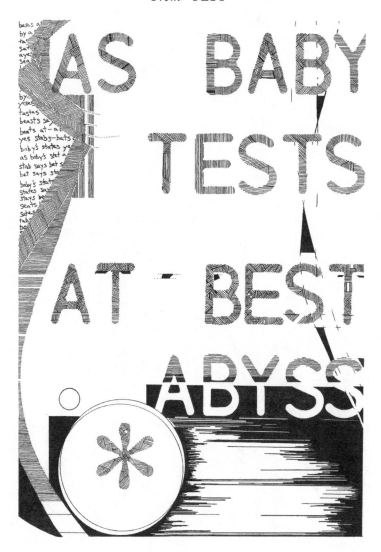

stunt,

If we

end it

anon,

stunt man, of him, an indoor Eiffel Tower,

I mourn,

for the

fflotsam.

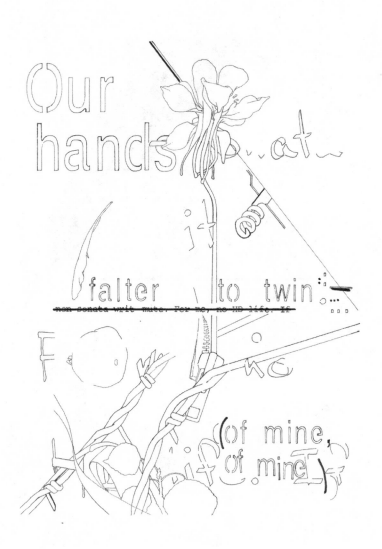

Our

hands that

if

falter to twin:..

non sonata writ mute. For me, no in life. If

F me

(of mine,
of mine)

FROM THE POETRY REVIEW

The fourth installment of our exchange with the Poetry Review.

A.K. BLAKEMORE

The flower is forever my captain

I think it should behave like the jeweler's name printed in high gloss
on the very white ring box as it is turned in the hand under the light,
or like the shape drawn in the condensation on a bus window early
in the morning but late enough for several other people to have come
and gone and fogged the shape with their breathing, or an extremely
recent snowfall that contains minuscule claw prints and a single pair
of boot prints that have no obvious beginning at a doorway in the
manner you would expect, or like scallops — and be treated accord-
ingly. The word *scallops* — which reminds me of *scalps* — which in
turn makes me think of a razor blade being taken to the softly furred
(why furred?) stomach of a female Neptune. Sometimes I come home
from work after dark and strip lights in my kitchen will not turn on
straight away, but instead flash abortively, and I stand in the hallway
turning the switch on and off as my black cat walks across the lino-
leum floor, and is visible only in these flashes, a few strides further at
each gasp of the light that will not work. And I think, that is how we
should move from one thing to another in a poem.

The first draft I wrote of this seemed more like *a short guide for
the female dilettante.* Now I intend to insist that all it is or can be is
a cotton throw whose pattern has been ruined after a thread in the
weft was tugged astray by a broken press-on nail. Identify where you
sit in this metaphor. I have suffered from visual and auditory hallu-
cinations since adolescence (sounding tones when lying in bed and
waking up, unknown voices that deliver bewildering imperatives, the
malevolent twitching of regular patterned surfaces, e.g. wallpapers
and kitchen tiles seen as though through a heat shimmer). This was
a gamma-mode life where some living room walls were an emerald
fern covered in swarming insects or particles of golden prelapsarian
dust that found form in the fading propulsion of a gust from the open
door of a different place where there were no living rooms. None
of this ever felt violent, or even particularly frightening. Some were
also just living room walls. This once fully convinced me of my own
divinity, or perhaps a form of Angelhood.

In practice, you start with a wash like one of the three or four
nights of distant and overlaying frost that come during the year. Look,

there is frost on the pampas grass and on the corner of the roof as well. You must shape from the silence the night shift walk home. A field of purity to be disturbed as little as possible. Early mornings are different on Saturday or Sunday, and this is a different kind of poem. Imagine you have sent a text message the reply to which might kill you — you will say to your friend later, *it killed me.* You are waiting for this reply. You bunch your fingers in your mouth and boil a kettle for something to do, pretending you are not waiting for this reply. That is the state, in front of the wash. Pay attention to the shape — horizontal lines are fattening. Some words are more beautiful than others and there is no shame in playing to this. There are many excellent poems about swans in part because of this. Snow both hides and makes apparent the below. To etch is to place shadow on a white space. Even children can do this.

> Poetry: Incursions of language into the daily.
>> In our polychrome, not color-happy dailiness,
>> the language of the poem, if it wants to remain the language of
>> the p., will by necessity be *gray.*
>> — From *Microliths* by Paul Celan, tr. Pierre Joris

Sometimes it begins with an uncharitable thought. Or rather, following an uncharitable thought upstream to the nasty spring. As much from that as from the tender observation that makes your heart buckle under its own weight. It is late evening in Farringdon and a girl ahead of me in the queue at the newsagent — a girl in an interesting woollen hat, who I assume is French — says to another girl who is with her: "The flower is forever my captain." She says this waving a bunch of wan, crinkled tulips. A different girl spills a Black Russian into the lap of a journalist who is wearing lemon-yellow tuxedo trousers. Tell me what you need to look at to survive. I find it helps to continue to think of writing as a delicious affectation that you are not hanging too much on. Another delicious affectation is to say you derive inspiration from the graceful silence of headstones, which I do. Headstones found in a rural graveyard that you took a spontaneous walk to in order to avoid your overbearing family. *Economy and resonance.* Women beat their slippers against the doorsteps late at night. Do they still?

Tenets are: All poetry is political but to write a poem is rarely a political act — accomplish those elsewhere. These poems are a form of ceasing to exist — they benefit from subtraction, not addition. Don't be too hard on yourself for being obscure: most of what we encounter in life defies exegesis, people are used to it. But there should be a cleanliness to it — a soapstone feel. "You want to write a sentence as clean as a bone. That is the goal," James Baldwin told the *Paris Review* in 1984. He was talking about prose, but I don't care.

If you are a woman, writing about your experience of being a woman, you are part of one of the most avant-garde literary movements there has ever been. Everything that happens in this poem is entirely your fault.

JACK UNDERWOOD

On Poetry and Uncertain Subjects

The game involved me or my brother climbing on top of something not too high, like a sofa, or a tree stump, and asking Dad to catch us. He would get into position and say, "Go on! Jump! I'll catch you," and every time we leapt, he'd back away and let us fall. We'd try it over and over, each time becoming more suspicious, demanding new assurances, squinting and giggling as we scrutinized his face. He'd be already laughing as he said it again, "Go on! Jump! I'll catch you." He never caught us, and never would catch us, and that, we understood, was the whole point.

What we loved about the game was precisely the feeling of be-ing unsure — the naïve, delicious, uncertain tension before the jump: maybe, maybe, maybe this time; even Dad must have wondered if he could hold his nerve indefinitely. Nowadays I get my uncertain tension-feelings most tangibly as a writer, and specifically as a person who writes poems. With poems you have to risk all kinds of small, hopeful, doomed leaps; uncertainty is central to your business. You not only have to acknowledge the innate inaccuracy of language as a system that cannot catch or hold onto anything securely, but also that it's precisely this characteristic of inaccuracy that a poetic, empathetic transaction rests on. Writing poems, you don't just look up from your computer screen every so often and remind yourself that endless re-interpretation threatens to destabilize each of the terms you are using, or that those terms are calibrated and reliant upon endless further terms, wobbling, drifting, and stunning each other like a huge shoal of jellyfish. Instead, you deliberately build your poem as an open habitation; you have to learn to leave holes in the walls, because you won't and can't be around later on to clear up any ambiguities when the lakes of your readers' lives come flooding up through the floor.

If a poem works it's because you've made it such that other people might participate in making it meaningful, and this participation will always rest on another person's understanding of the poem and its relationship to a world that is not your own. Your own understand-ing of the poem will evolve over time too, as you reread it in light of your changing world, just as you will find the world altered in light of the poem you wrote to understand a small uncertain corner of it.

With poems, you never get to settle on a final meaning for your work, just as you never get to feel settled, finally, as yourself. So it seems entirely natural to me that poets, exploring and nudging such unstable material, foregrounding connotation and metaphor, and constantly dredging up the gunk of unconscious activity over which they have no control, might start to doubt the confidence, finality, and the general big-bearded Victorian arrogance of certainty as it seems to appear in other forms of language: mathematical, religious, political, legal, or financial. I've reached a point now where I'm so used to accepting how flimsily language in poems relates to the world that I can't help but feel appalled at the hapless trust we place in other kinds of language elsewhere. Surely all of meaning and knowledge is apprehended, expressed, and configured unstably, is just as much a shoal of jellyfish? Surely we should be uncertain about practically everything?

> Before the beginning — unknown.
> As after the end — unknown.
> But floating, stretched between,
>
> the mind's harmonic mappings,
> frail as gossamer,
> *costing not less than everything.*
>
> I am alive. I'm human.
> Get dressed. Make coffee.
> Shore a few lines against my ruin.

That's Anne Stevenson, at the end of her long poem *A Lament for the Makers*, which imagines that hell is only for poets. "Before the beginning — unknown./As after the end — unknown." This idea of an overall, timeless uncertainty is not new, by any means, especially when it comes to poetry and different philosophies of language. Poststructuralism in particular has had this covered for over fifty years, and I've waded uncertainly through enough of that to know the limits of my own understanding. Elsewhere, feminist theory has exposed how the Western history of human knowledge has been dominated by white, male knowers, making our so-called "universal claims" according to finalized, standardized terms, spoken from our supposedly "objective" perspectives, as if somehow our minds pertained toward a special clarity and coolness, like water fresh from the fridge.

Scholars and critics might conclude that the uncertainty of language has been so commonly theorized that revisiting how poems work according to this same uncertain quality is merely "re-inventing the wheel." But these are our working conditions as poets; uncertainty is our predicament, and we are compelled to reconsider it in our work all the time. And anyway, "re-inventing the wheel" is a pretty good analogy for our business; we are always weighing our egoism against the poems that precede us, staring down our insignificance, shoring a few lines in spite of it. So it's writing poems, not reading theory, that makes me wonder if the empathetic negotiation of meaning between poets and readers, which is innate to the effectiveness of poetry, is also a dynamic feature of other fields.

In her "Short Lecture on Socrates," the poet Mary Ruefle introduces Socrates's "only true wisdom": "knowing that you know nothing." She writes:

> I am forever telling my students I know nothing about poetry, and they never believe me. I do not know what my poems are about, except on rare occasions, and I never know what they mean. I have met and spoken to many poets who feel the same way, and one among them once put it this way: "The difference between myself and a student is that I am better at not knowing what I am doing." I couldn't put it any better than that if I tried.

We all encounter stalling moments of uncertainty when the strategies we have developed for ourselves and each other fail to console the overwhelming complexity and unpredictability of being alive with everything else on earth. At these times we tend to look upwards in the hope that God, or the seemingly omniscient physics of the universe, will disclose to us the Truth, the reason, the theory, its ointment:

> *Please*: a word so short
> it could get lost in the air
> as it floats up to God like the feather it is,
> knocking and knocking, and finally
> falling back to earth as rain,
> as pellets of ice, soaking a black branch,
> collecting in drains, leaching into the ground,
> and you walk in that weather every day.
> — From *The Word That Is a Prayer* by Ellery Akers

What interests me about poetry is that rather than looking up for answers, it tends to lead us back indoors, to the mirror, as if seeing ourselves reflected within its frame, confused, gawping, empty-eyed, and scalded by circumstance, might re-teach us the lesson: that meaning presents itself precisely as a question — therefore, you can't entertain it by seeking to answer it. Imagine! The old, old universe, arranging itself legibly into a puzzle that our small brains might be qualified to solve with the knowledge we can accrue from our small corner of its tablecloth. Solving the mysteries of the universe: isn't that just the most arrogant, preposterous thing you ever heard? The idea of there being some sort of Answer to Everything is an admirable feat of imagination but also displays a woeful lack of it.

But poems use language so unstably they remind us that the concept of meaning in the universe belongs only to us, and not, in fact, to the universe itself. Meaning is a human beloved: we are *literally made for each other*; no one understands us like we do. So it's as a poet that I feel relatively qualified in my not knowing, and my knowing I don't know, because I spend so much time within that odd intellectual hollow, where words will always fail me. Like Ruefle, I also teach poetry for a living, so I guess I am also in the business of teaching my students not to know, and teaching them to understand how and why they cannot know, and to regard this as the "only true wisdom," that is, to see not knowing as a crucial advancement of knowledge. It's really the only kind of knowledge we were born with, and we spend our lives forgetting and remembering it.

But this argument is very abstract; it's got no things in it, and things are of great importance and interest. Of things, Jung says, "if a man does not know what a thing *is*, it is at least an increase in knowledge if he knows what it is *not*," which is one of those quotes that feels very helpful, but also, immediately, not helpful at all. Jung's things are too abstract as well. But we can take from this, by implication, that poetry, unburdened by the need to demonstrate knowledge in a way that is quantifiable or provable, is free to explore the world of things in a way that relies just as much on dissonance or absence as coherence, or evidence. In poems, the foggier aspects of language, which most of the time we ignore or squint through in order to swap workable sentences with one another, are instead called upon deliberately to blur things, to describe things Impressionistically; from across the room a sentence might denote a bridge, a pond, some water lilies, but up close, as it is in poems, language becomes paint again: gestural,

layered; the awareness of illusion is part of the effect —

> Here is where an afternoon eats its meal from the hollow
> of elbow pits.
>
> — From *Asmara Road, NW2* by Momtaza Mehri

Poetry is a deliberate act of foregrounding language, smudging it, to signal possible meanings beyond the everyday, sharper constraints that words and sentences usually afford us, or rather, we afford to them. We know that language is being foregrounded in poetry because often enough we can recognize a poem immediately on the page. Poems tend to announce or frame themselves, either as discrete items surrounded by white space, or else by some other unusual formal arrangement. Form is part of the ceremonial dress code, as if language is putting on some nice white robes to mark itself out as different from the congregation, or it's like in films when people recede on a dance floor to form a circle, making room for someone who has something specific to say by their dancing. With the exception of the poems that deploy a prose line, usually the page recedes from around a poem, making extra room for the spatial specifics of its performance. But poems foreground their uncertain language in less visible ways as well.

Usually we tend to read texts in a single direction (left to right, top to bottom, in the case of most Western languages) and poems also appear to take place in this same predictable sequence, aside from some notable Modernist or avant-garde exceptions. We are encouraged to trust the standard technology of a sentence, even when it's chopped up into lines, or musically interrupted by great clanging rhymes every ten syllables. But if we look closely it becomes clear that poetic language often operates against the sequential logic of the sentence it inhabits and comprises. For example, when Plath compares her father to a "bag full of God," she asks that the properties of both the father and the bag full of God be examined simultaneously, interchangeably. The words stay fixed in their position in the sentence, but the mind hops back and forth, overlapping the ideas that the words assign, smudging their meanings out of order. The act of comparison, central to poetic thought, antedates the sequential logic of a sentence.

Then there's the fact that poems are commonly held to be rereadable objects, so the whole longer sequence of the poem gets played over, looped, layered, taken out of order; the sustain pedal is held down until the individual notes become the one great chord of the thing, reverberating. Metaphor, symbolism, music, irony: connotation floods the banks of a sentence so naturally and regularly that language must surely have evolved with these extra breaching, poetic qualities as integral to its working. Without this propensity to overflow, any act of communication would be stunted, cold, robotic, and yet we hardly ever credit this unstable stuff with making knowledge possible, but tend to insist instead that ideas are most clearly communicated through orderly syntax, correct grammar, a breadth and specificity of vocabulary. The epistemic value of poetry has been shunted way down the pecking order. You may as well cough into a hedge and wait for a fact to fall out, that's how our culture feels about poetic knowledge.

It is very romantic to be a poet ... like having a bad back ...

But it is also a pleasure ... like squeezing your legs together ... and buttoning your blouse all the way up ...

But then it is too much pleasure, like peach pie

And it becomes ... too average to live ...

That's Chelsey Minnis, from her book *Bad Bad*, in which she also says things like, "Poetry is made to produce an expensive drowsiness ... /With a true flickering of disinterest ... " or "When I write a poem it's like looking through a knothole into a velvet fuckpad ... " If you accrue knowledge through Minnis's poems then it is untethered, fractious, annoyed at being made to sit still. It's a knowledge that wants you to quit being so grabby all the time. An uncertain knowledge. Or take this, from Morgan Parker's "The World Is Beautiful but You Are Not in It":

> I am getting close
> enough to the sun to touch the tip of its cigar.
>
> We carry what is shocking and heavy in blood.
> Music seems brighter: the sky the sky.

What to do with a sky that is itself twice over? You can't paraphrase or simplify the complexity of this speaker's predicament. You can't know the shock and weight of the knowledge they carry; instead it's kept bloody, hidden. But this is not the kind of hiding or confusion of elements that shuts you out. It gets you wondering, doing the imaginative hard work of empathy, the heat of that sun, its cigar-tip crackling, the sky doubly wide open, and something shocking, mortal, weighing down on a collective memory of trauma. Can you feel it? Can you understand? Almost. Maybe. Not something definite, but definitely something.

This is the kind of uncertain knowledge made possible in poems. I don't mean uncertainty as indecision, but as a philosophical, empathetic stance: I am uncertain. Most poems take this stance in one way or another, and of course there is a wider avant-garde tradition and conceptual field of poetics where meaning in a text can be viewed as a secondary or entirely incidental feature of its construction. But what these various poetries have in common is a resistance to finality in language, and to the kind of certain knowledge that shuts down revision or discussion, or suggests that knowledge can't also be (say it) *felt*.

But it can't just be poems where uncertain knowledge is openly recognized as productive and beneficial. I am sure that if we look we will find that every field of thought employs language that either includes poetic features, or else lives in denial of the inevitable gap that must exist between the word and the thing; it's just that with poetry, and art in general, we are encouraged to feel safe enough in our uncertainty to admit the "true wisdom" of not knowing to ourselves. If we look at humankind's moth-like progress toward the front porch light of knowledge it is typified not by the subtraction of falsehoods to a single strand of Truth, not by a reductive fundamentalism, but by the production of more and more gestures of certainty in different directions. More and more versions of Truth, more and more sources of light on the porch.

We can choose to ignore the noise of other people's certainties with a close-minded conviction in attending to our own; we can rig up a contraption of agreement and say we all see it one way, pretending that there is not enough discrepancy in the small print of our subjectivities to prove this a lie, or we can simply admit that Truth in the Universe Knowable to Humankind is really a great diversification of certainties, crystallizing endlessly away from a mythical absolute. Knowledge is, at very best, infinitely Venn diagrammatic. If art has anything like a duty to the rest of human thought, perhaps it is to remind us that the more versions of the Truth we declare, the less absolutely true our Truth can be.

And since I'm already on my horse, and am prone to finding advantages, I might also suggest that poetry, that oft-maligned, wafty corner of dynamic not-knowing, that shadowy Hamlet mooning around on his platform at midnight, strung out, self-effacing, and spoken to by ghosts, should be acknowledged as the prime medium for the articulation of our knowledge of the unknown.

Uncertain knowledge is declared and revealed everywhere in poetry: "the glass and salt my crooked pathway; impassable glass and salt," writes Rachael Allen impassably in her poem "Kingdomland"; "we talk about how weird it is/to be 'a thing,'" writes Stacey Teague in "it becomes a part of—," and I guess Jung would say that this "is at least an increase in knowledge," while Chloe Stopa-Hunt explains in "Harbour-Chapel" that "We all decode our blows: *What light is,/ What vessel, what heart is,*" and we can only feel our way to believing her strangely, as we feel our way to strangely believing Don Mee Choi, who writes in "Weaver in Exile," "Dear Father, I am sitting on crows' backs that wobble with grease. Stars look like pebbles from here." And E.E. Cummings, what does he have to say about it all?

> what's beyond logic happens beneath will
> ....
> since the thing perhaps is
> to eat flowers and not to be afraid.
> — From *[voices to voices, lip to lip]*

Eat the flowers and do not be afraid — of uncertainty, of doubt — that seems key; that seems to be what poems are proof of: a fearlessness toward, or defiance against the profound inaccuracy of our perceived reality and relation to it. In "Of the Surface of Things," Wallace Stevens writes: "In my room, the world is beyond my understanding;/But when I walk I see that it consists of three or four hills and a cloud." Of course, he's oversimplifying things to show us, by the inadequacy of his limited scenery, the impossibility of the task in hand, the task of trying to describe what it's like being alive in the world. Oof! It hurts your guts just thinking about it. But then, being brave, staring it down if only for a moment, you can tell yourself what Sophie Robinson does, so restoratively, in "Hurtface (after Ceravolo)":

> o bum! o joy! o bloated world!
>> what dreams i am on the stairs of!

Sometimes I get a whooshing-out feeling, a kind of abstraction or self-consciousness about being, especially in large groups of people. I don't think this is unusual. I'm pretty sure most people get feelings of sudden distance from their surroundings for no apparent reason, but with friends, having a nice time, this distance can be entirely pleasurable, sublime even. Someone I love will be talking, or dancing with someone else I love, and in a way I can only describe as cinematic, the volume, or context, drops, and there it all is, this unstable, miraculous wad. I realize I have no answer for it, nothing to say, no conclusion to draw, and yes, I feel something like tranquility, but also awe, a happy, overwhelming fear. The lack of an explanation for all the wide mad fuss of the world only makes it the bigger miracle: "How — I didn't know any / word for it — how 'unlikely' ... " as Elizabeth Bishop puts it in her poem "In the Waiting Room":

> I said to myself: three days
> and you'll be seven years old.
> I was saying it to stop
> the sensation of falling off
> the round, turning world,
> into cold, blue-black space.

What tethers us down seems so plainly tenuous, so "unlikely," that I think every now and then we should want to fall into that "cold, blue-black space." It seems so arrogant to dismiss its emptiness as unremunerative, or mistake it for an impasse. We know that there's nothing to be found out there, but we can still feel ourselves standing upon the precarious ledge of an inconsolable question together. In poems we can look down at the sheer, deathy drop of it. "Go on! Jump! I'll catch you."

VAHNI CAPILDEO

Punishable Bodies: Poetry on the Offensive

"You don't understand how offensive this poetry is," I held myself back from saying. "No, please, wait. This poetry would offend a lot of people. It has the capacity to do that. Don't applaud it until or unless you understand that."

We were four poets: Gregory Pardlo, Shivanee Ramlochan, Natalie Diaz, and myself. We had met in New York for "Poetry and Desire: A Reading and Conversation," cosponsored by Poets House and the PEN World Voices Festival. It was early summer. Ramlochan had just finished reading from her first book, *Everyone Knows I Am a Haunting*. In her poetry, there are abortionists; "cross-dressers"; rape survivors who accuse the police and invoke Shakespeare; multi-gendered women-born, whose sexual desires are expressed in images of attack and dismemberment: an abundance of queer personae. The audience, sitting with their backs to the plate glass that gave onto the darkening streets, feasted on the richness and bravery of it. We writers sat looking out at them, and into the night that seemed not so much falling on us as being pulled up from the river.

> Don't say forced anal entry.
> Say you learned that some flowers bloom and die
> at night. Say you remember stamen, filament,
> cross-pollination, say that hummingbirds are
>
> vital to the process.
> — From *On the Third Anniversary of the Rape*

What was the problem? Was there a problem?

It is a truism that poetry, transferred from one place to another, gains or loses in its power to offend, or its vulnerability to being deemed offensive. This truism becomes striking when the experience of that transfer is lived.

Those not "from" the Caribbean diaspora may not be aware of the infighting that is breaking out sporadically, in real and virtual spaces, over what is "authentically" Caribbean. Just after the historical moment of independence, now that the archipelago has begun speaking to as well as of itself, giant bell jars have started being clamped down upon it, empty yet already echoing with imported divisiveness, ethnic and otherwise. Writers who were peers have fallen out; some refuse to be in the same room, let alone mentor or review each other. People — poets — write, read, and are offended.

Caribbean literature may be at risk of "defining" itself according to the community battle lines, grant-awarding criteria, and teaching requirements of cold-climate eyes. Such a self-redefinition would have its costs. The loss would come at world literature's expense, with the near extinction of an older, continuous, and differently diverse archipelagic heritage, as ventriloquized and refreshed by writers who cannot be pinned down, mocking shape-shifters, Mercutio mashed up with Macbeth, laughing in the face of death, ironizing and creolizing faster than any online ordering site can be clicked.

So what was the problem I felt — perhaps nobody else did — at this particular reading?

It was as if the bass on a sound system had been turned too soft. Was Ramlochan's poetry sounding out as it should — disturbing the heart's function, not just thrilling or pleasing it? The scope and foci of her writing are deeply and subtly offensive, both to the internationally marketed "Caribbean woman" image, and to the strand of conservatism at home in the region (and not without its mirrors or twins elsewhere).

The first offense is simple. "Caribbean poetry," massaged into a recognizable "identity" for international book sales and programs, abounds in the bodies of women: lush, dripping, papaya-like females, beautifully rebellious fuckers; their wise, dried-up, once-fruity grandmothers, maybe politicians' mistresses but depicted as witches; culturally appropriate, or appropriated, ghosts snapped out of recent agricultural labor, or colonization's early massacres; perhaps the occasional petticoated prophetess speaking in tongues, or a schoolyard oppressor armed with a yardstick. Representative women — the canon is still too new for them to be stereotypical women — are devilish and/or nurturing, innocent and/or wry. By contrast, Ramlochan's characters are not the expected or rewarded characters, and her "nature imagery" is subversively deployed. Ramlochan's personae flip as soon as you think you recognize them. They are equally unlikely to gratify the reader by offering themselves for incorporation in exotic copulation fantasies or in earthy ancestral yearnings. They are articulate and shameless about their dissonance and extremes, refusing to oppose or reconcile intellect and desire, embeddedness and travel, home and away. They would be difficult to summarize, except by forced assimilations.

Perhaps this offense — against the formation of identity — will melt away in the reception of Ramlochan's volume. With any luck, the unconscious essentialist bias of every reader who *just feels this is not quite the right fit* and therefore does not review, buy, or shortlist the book will be offset by ten others who *feel this is just what we have needed for a long time* — though statistical precedent for such a positive response does not exist.

The second offense is less simple, and does not seem modern. However, how often, and in how few ways, and as heard by whom, does the actuality of modernity resemble the stories that "modernity" tells itself about itself? Ramlochan raises subjects that are taboo. This is a question of content, not form or angle. The events in her book belong in the kind of conversations that women, or LGBT+ persons, or field workers, or fourth-generation almost-Hindus, or any other "subaltern" or "alternative" group, have amongst themselves and would absolutely never publish. Such stories are dirty linen and desperation's prayer flags. These are not the stories that keep up with the neighbors. They are dangerous ammunition for "the other side," the always potential enemy who might well also be a loving part of the family, or chairing the Commission of Enquiry, or influencing the appointments committee. This is not a matter of etiquette but of life and death, in societies that have resisted examination of their transgenerational normalizations of cruelties, and for all of us, as messy individuals within the framework of reasonable civil behavior as constructed by law.

We are created equal under law, but laws are not equal. Legal codes figure among the "languages" against, and within, and beside which the crafted language of poetry makes itself heard; even if we choose to, or are privileged to, ignore this harsher framework which holds us. In February 2016, in the Christian liturgical season of Lent, the body of a visiting Japanese musician was found behind a tree in a popular and central green space of Trinidad's capital, Port of Spain. The steel pannist had been murdered during Carnival, possibly by someone known to her, but there were few clues to the circumstances. The mayor of the city took this as the occasion to denounce, more than once, the "vulgarity and lewdness" that women have the "responsibility" to "enjoy Carnival without." His speech was far from poetic: "It's a matter of, if she was still in her costume — I think that's what I heard — let your imagination roll." This sparked protests, and the mayor resigned. The protesters were met by counter-protesters, many female (and not a hired crowd), who supported the mayor: identity-politickers practicing "whataboutery" — why fuss over a relatively pale-skinned foreigner when our own are missing; and self-appointed enforcers of sexual mores, supposedly focused on women's dignity. This happened in a nation that prides itself on its "culture" — while permitting child marriage, restricting and partially criminalizing reproductive rights, and (like at least seventy-five countries worldwide) making homosexuality an offense.

Ramlochan's transgressive poems are not, or not only, about self-fashioning for the sake of self-discovery or self-expression. They have grown up in blood and soil that create bodies as glittering yet punishable, which make the human turn metamorphic, transformed under excessive heat and pressure. When they are in drag, drag is also dread.

Nine days before the Poets House reading, Ramlochan had performed her work under the glitter ball and rainbow flag of the Euphoria Lounge in Port of Spain, at the Bocas Lit Fest's "Lit: On Fleek" showcase "for emergent and established LGBT writers." There, in a contained party atmosphere, a bubble in that context of a homeland where affirmation and condemnation lurch in a seemingly forever tango, her words felt tentative as well as powerful, in a way that was not quite the same as in New York: endangered as well as dangerous, on the offensive as well as suffering offense. For poetry and offense is give and take, as well as reread, misread, place, displace, and replace.

Sudden, invisible, American light interrupted the Poets House Q&A. Fireworks were going off. They boomed, in immense quantity, reminding us of the immensity of the city that we were in. That day, President Donald Trump was paying a visit to New York. The next day would be the Mexican-American celebration of Cinco de Mayo. Which of these wildly differing occasions was being marked? The booming continued. We imagined explosions of color somewhere in the sky. Had something entirely different happened? A triumph or disaster — and for whom? The air in the room was thick with unpre-dictability. We had to halt the Q&A, and observe a jittery, chattering half-silence. It was like crowd-sourcing tension; like a flash mob of apprehension. A column of people in Star Wars gear, mostly white males, carrying lightsabers like real offensive weapons, laughed their way, soundlessly to us, down the pavement. Who were they for or against? With what might their light-heartedness align? Did it have intention? Would it turn into action?

Right there in Manhattan, it began to seem possible that in a generation or so, Ramlochan's poetry might have regained its power to offend in the "first world," in un-Caribbean countries, which are cutting back on human rights. In fact, should such a day come — not unforeseeably — not just her book but her brown body might be banned from circulation.

Half a lie can do more damage than a thoroughgoing lie. One half-lie in circulation at the time of writing is that "political correctness" — the corrective to the public and private derogation, i.e. the normalized abuse, meted out to the less powerful — and related practices, such as questioning why those who can buy media attention to incite violence should be invited to share the platform when debates are conducted in learning environments, are so offensive to self-identified free-thinkers and allegedly disenfranchised non-minorities, that such attempts at more civilized discourse should be targeted as the cause of prejudicial behavior against those who have requested respect by these and other means. Curiously, there is less attention given to those who might ask whether truth and reconciliation commissions, or educational programs, might be needed to clear the air, not to mention the hearts and minds, amongst those who are the natural inheritors of the transgenerational attitudes that thrived in lands acquired by murder and enriched through slavery. That statement would cause offense. It also might not fit in the type of poem that gains a "platform."

"Offense," as an abstract noun, is an odd word in the constructions that home it. In English, offense may be taken or given. In emotional truth, offense may balloon around full of poison gas, leaking and punctured, but not owned — and with a trailing string. Sometimes it drops like a mis-launched firework. If I am — if one is — aware of an intention to offend, a space may open up where distance can be taken; the offense can be dodged or coolly allowed to go flying; and the intention, or the ill-wisher, be dealt with rationally. It is possible to have a detached response. When one's life is not immediately at stake, or dependent on the whimsical mercy of overpowering forces, that is.

People are good at feeling what they ought to feel: at catching a communal emotion, and letting it carry them away; or at carrying through with whatever action that communal emotion may move them toward, or justify, or apparently require. In extreme yet not uncommon cases, where a poet has been disappeared, killed, jailed, tortured, banned, or terrorized into compliance with the state or some other dominant grouping, how many good citizens — if compelled to attend a reading of the offending poems, a recitation of words, no body to punish — would feel personally offended, upset to their core? How many would have suspended a personal self in favor of a collective self, in a kind of internal keeping up with imagined and cruel neighbors? In aligning themselves under the banner of anger, instead of experiencing offense, might they not be the opposite of upset — in tidying away a supposed threat, perhaps they might feel righteous, strong, and strengthened? Even in the case of "blasphemy," is the condemnation really for the what (let alone the how) of saying — is the poem condemned? Or is it the poet who is condemned, for the temerity of speaking out of turn?

Poetry, and offense, are both personal and impersonal. Foisting a documentary, rather than imaginative, duty on the poet at work, and marketing poetry by encouraging the identification of the work with the ocular proof of the poet in body, rather than expanding the role and responsibilities of the audience, is perhaps not the most clarifying — or inoffensive — move for literature today.

CONTRIBUTORS

HANIF ABDURRAQIB* is the author of *They Can't Kill Us Until They Kill Us* (Two Dollar Radio, 2017).

RAYMOND ANTROBUS is the author of *The Perseverance* (Penned in the Margins, 2018) and *To Sweeten Bitter* (Out-Spoken Press, 2017). He's a freelance spoken word and poetry teacher who lives in London.

NOAH BALDINO's* poems and reviews are forthcoming in *Kenyon Review*, *Black Warrior Review*, and elsewhere. They teach in Indiana.

CHASE BERGGRUN* is the author of *R E D* (Birds, LLC, 2018). They live and work in New York City.

A.K. BLAKEMORE's* second full-length collection, *Fondue*, will be published by Offord Road Books this July.

VAHNI CAPILDEO* is the author of *Venus as a Bear* (Carcanet Press, 2018). They are the Douglas Caster Cultural Fellow in Poetry at the University of Leeds.

EDUARDO C. CORRAL teaches in the MFA program at North Carolina State University in Raleigh. He's currently a Hodder Fellow at Princeton University.

MATTHEW DICKMAN's* most recent collection of poetry is *Wonderland* (W.W. Norton, 2018).

PHILIP GOOD's* new chapbook is *Poets in a Box* (Reality Beach, 2018).

JOEL LIPMAN was appointed as the first Lucas County Poet Laureate in 2008. He is an Emeritus Professor of English and founded ABRACADABRA Studio of Poetics.

DORA MALECH's third book of poetry, *Stet*, is forthcoming from Princeton University Press in 2018, and her fourth, *Flourish*, is forthcoming from Carnegie Mellon University Press in 2020.

BERNADETTE MAYER's most recent book, *Works and Days* (New Directions, 2016), was a National Book Critics Circle Award finalist.

HENRI MICHAUX (1899–1984) was a Belgian-born French poet, painter, and mental traveler into the inner worlds revealed by dreams, myths, and psychedelic drugs. "Postface" is from *Plume* by Henri Michaux © Editions Gallimard, 1963. Translation © Richard Sieburth, 2018. Published in English by NYRB Poets.

KRISTEN RENEE MILLER* is an editor and director of educational programming at Sarabande Books.

D.A. POWELL's books include *Repast* (2014) and *Useless Landscape, or A Guide for Boys* (2012), both from Graywolf Press.

RICHARD SIEBURTH is the translator of Gershom Scholem's *Greetings from Angelus* (Archipelago Books, 2018) and Henri Michaux's *A Certain Plume* (New York Review Books, 2018).

KINGA TÓTH is the author of *Moonlight Faces* (Magvető, 2017). She is a writer, translator, visual and sound poet, and performer who lives between Germany and Hungary.

JACK UNDERWOOD is the author of *Happiness* (Faber & Faber, 2015). He teaches at Goldsmiths College, University of London.

JENNY XIE is the author of *Eye Level* (Graywolf Press, 2018). She teaches at New York University.

---

* First appearance in *Poetry*.

POETRY

ARE YOU LISTENING?

POETRY FOUNDATION
MAY FEATURES

POETRY PODCASTS	**POETRY MAGAZINE PODCAST** *Poetry* editors **Don Share** and **Lindsay Garbutt** talk to contributors and share their poem selections from this issue with listeners. **POETRY OFF THE SHELF** Producer **Curtis Fox** explores the diverse world of contemporary American poetry through readings and interviews. **POETRYNOW** May's four-minute episodes feature new poems by **Nick Twemlow, Anjuli Fatima Raza Kolb, John Lennox**, and **Mary Cisper**. Produced in partnership with the WFMT Radio Network. **VS PODCAST** **Danez Smith** and **Franny Choi** host a bi-weekly series where poets confront the ideas that move them. Produced by **Daniel Kisslinger**, and presented in partnership with Postloudness. May guest poets include **Kaveh Akbar, Angel Nafis**, and **Safia Elhillo**. Podcasts are available free from the iTunes store and on poetryfoundation.org.
HARRIET BLOG	May's featured blogger **Joel Craig** discusses poetry, craft, and the writing life of a poet at poetryfoundation.org/harriet.
POETRY FOUNDATION .ORG	Visit poetryfoundation.org to browse our database of more than 40,000 poems, including the entire *Poetry* archive, or to listen to the *Poetry* magazine podcast, read contributor biographies and blog posts, or catch up on the latest issue online.
EVENTS	Plan your trip to Chicago to see some of our May events! *Poetry off the Shelf* **MARK DOTY & RAFAEL CAMPO** Thursday, May 10, 7:00 PM Poetry Foundation *Poetry off the Shelf* **GHOST FISHING: AN ECO-JUSTICE POETRY ANTHOLOGY** Thursday, May 24, 7:00 PM Poetry Foundation *Poetry & Music* **ZAFA COLLECTIVE** Friday, May 31, 7:00 PM Poetry Foundation
EXHIBITION	**BETTISSIMA: TREASURES FROM THE POETS HOUSE ELIZABETH KRAY ARCHIVES** April 3 – May 30, 2018; Monday – Friday, 11:00 AM – 4:00 PM

POETRY FOUNDATION
61 West Superior Steet
Chicago, Illinois 60654
poetryfoundation.org

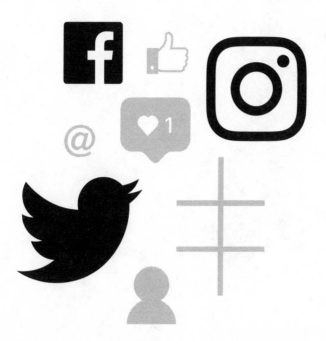

POETRY

ARE YOU FOLLOWING US?

f @poetryfoundation
🐦 @poetryfound @poetrymagazine
📷 @poetryfoundation

Subscribe to POETRY today and receive a free tote!

Print subscription comes with complimentary digital access.

poetryfoundation.org/subscribe